T0070450

SELF-ASSESSMENT

REALITY-BASED LEADERSHIP

CY WAKEMAN

From *The New York Times* Best-Selling Author of
The Reality-Based Rules of the Workplace

WILEY

Copyright © 2014 by John Wiley & Sons, Inc. All Rights Reserved.

Published by Wiley

One Montgomery Street, Suite 1200, San Francisco, CA 94104-4594

www.wiley.com

Cover image: Thinkstock

Cover design: Adrian Morgan

No part of this publication may be reproduced, stored in a retrieval system, or transmitted in any form or by any means, electronic, mechanical, photocopying, recording, scanning, or otherwise, except as permitted under Section 107 or 108 of the 1976 United States Copyright Act, without either the prior written permission of the Publisher, or authorization through payment of the appropriate per-copy fee to the Copyright Clearance Center, Inc., 222 Rosewood Drive, Danvers, MA 01923, 978-750-8400, fax 978-646-8600, or on the web at www.copyright.com. Requests to the Publisher for permission should be addressed to the Permissions Department, John Wiley & Sons, Inc., 111 River Street, Hoboken, NJ 07030, 201-748-6011, fax 201-748-6008, or online at http://www.wiley.com/go/permissions.

Limit of Liability/Disclaimer of Warranty: While the publisher and author have used their best efforts in preparing this book, they make no representations or warranties with respect to the accuracy or completeness of the contents of this book and specifically disclaim any implied warranties of merchantability or fitness for a particular purpose. No warranty may be created or extended by sales representatives or written sales materials. The advice and strategies contained herein may not be suitable for your situation. You should consult with a professional where appropriate. Neither the publisher nor author shall be liable for any loss of profit or any other commercial damages, including but not limited to special, incidental, consequential, or other damages. Readers should be aware that Internet websites offered as citations and/or sources for further information may have changed or disappeared between the time this was written and when it is read.

For additional copies/bulk purchases of this book in the U.S. please contact 800-274-4434.

For additional copies or bulk purchases of this book or to learn more about Wiley's Workplace Learning offerings, please contact us toll free at 1-866-888-5159 or by email at workplacelearning@wiley.com .

Wiley also publishes its books in a variety of electronic formats and by print-on-demand. Some material included with standard print versions of this book may not be included in e-books or in print-on-demand. If the version of this book that you purchased references media such as a CD or DVD that was not included in your purchase, you may download this material at http://booksupport.wiley.com. For more information about Wiley products, visit www.wiley.com.

ISBN: 978-1-118-54046-6

Printed in the United States of America

Printing SKY65BE9A66-EF63-4E0E-83FD-DA5E11AB3C1B_063023

Instructions

Below you will find twenty-four statements that describe dimensions of leadership behavior. Read each statement carefully and then circle the number that best reflects the degree to which you agree or disagree with that statement. Every statement must have a rating.

1 = Completely Disagree

2 = Mostly Disagree

3 = Somewhat Disagree

4 = Somewhat Agree

5 = Mostly Agree

6 = Completely Agree

1. The difference between success and failure is commitment.

   1 2 3 4 5 6

2. Decision-makers should take my opinion into account when making their decisions.

   1 2 3 4 5 6

3. Employees need to be given ample time to buy in to changes in the organization.

   1 2 3 4 5 6

4. I regularly participate in development experiences that are not funded by or arranged by my organization.

   1 2 3 4 5 6

5. Most employees have more influence on their supervisors than they think they do.

   1 2 3 4 5 6

Reality-Based Leadership: Self-Assessment. Copyright © 2014 by John Wiley & Sons, Inc.

1 = Completely Disagree
2 = Mostly Disagree
3 = Somewhat Disagree
4 = Somewhat Agree
5 = Mostly Agree
6 = Completely Agree

6. I consider myself active in social networking.

   1 2 3 4 5 6

7. When I consider issues that have prevented me from achieving positive results, I regularly identify things I could have done differently to change the outcome.

   1 2 3 4 5 6

8. My manager should provide me all the information and direction I need to do my job.

   1 2 3 4 5 6

9. I love receiving suggestions for how to do my job better.

   1 2 3 4 5 6

10. An individual is responsible for learning what he or she needs to be successful.

    1 2 3 4 5 6

11. Co-workers owe it to each other to offer suggestions for improvement.

    1 2 3 4 5 6

12. Success or failure often depends on how many obstacles there are in the way (that is, resource constraints, customer expectations, etc.).

    1 2 3 4 5 6

13. Doing more than what's expected is the key to getting ahead in life.

    1 2 3 4 5 6

14. Taking credit and accepting blame are equally important.

    1 2 3 4 5 6

Reality-Based Leadership: Self-Assessment. Copyright © 2014 by John Wiley & Sons, Inc.

1 = Completely Disagree

2 = Mostly Disagree

3 = Somewhat Disagree

4 = Somewhat Agree

5 = Mostly Agree

6 = Completely Agree

15. The main difference between success and failure is luck.

    1 2 3 4 5 6

16. My co-workers' behavior prevents me from doing my best work.

    1 2 3 4 5 6

17. When an employee has a problem, his or her manager should try to fix it.

    1 2 3 4 5 6

18. Most of what happens at work is out of my control.

    1 2 3 4 5 6

19. My past failures have prepared me to succeed in the future.

    1 2 3 4 5 6

20. It is acceptable for an employee's personal life to affect his or her performance at work.

    1 2 3 4 5 6

21. A person's ability to deal with change is determined by his or her personality and is therefore difficult to influence.

    1 2 3 4 5 6

22. Employees should be consulted on decisions that are going to affect them.

    1 2 3 4 5 6

23. It is inevitable to be in a bad mood at work some days.

    1 2 3 4 5 6

24. When I am frustrated, it is due to situations or circumstances outside my control.

    1 2 3 4 5 6

Reality-Based Leadership: Self-Assessment. Copyright © 2014 by John Wiley & Sons, Inc.

Reality-Based Leadership Profile Scoring

Instructions

1. Transfer the answers (numbers) you gave for each item to the scoring framework below. Note that the items are not in sequential order.
2. Add the numbers in each column and write the sum in the space provided.

Column A	Column B
1. _____	2. _____
4. _____	3. _____
5. _____	8. _____
6. _____	12. _____
7. _____	15. _____
9. _____	16. _____
10. _____	17. _____
11. _____	18. _____
13. _____	20. _____
14. _____	21. _____
19. _____	22. _____
	23. _____
	24. _____

SUM Column A: _____ **SUM Column B:** _____

Reality-Based Leadership: Self-Assessment. Copyright © 2014 by John Wiley & Sons, Inc.

Reality-based leaders have a score in Column A of 50 or higher and a score in Column B of 25 or less. If your score is different, don't despair. The Reality-Based Leadership Workshop is for you! If you are in alignment, that is good news.

In the Reality-Based Leadership Workshop, we will discuss non-conventional leadership practices that typically resonate with leaders and help them improve their business results. You will learn why some common approaches to the statements in this assessment actually create drama and hinder results. The Reality-Based Leadership Workshop will help you live from a more accountable context and be an example for others.

Reality-Based Leadership: Self-Assessment. Copyright © 2014 by John Wiley & Sons, Inc.

Discover more at www.wiley.com

WILEY

ISBN 978-1-118-54046-6